THE NAVAJO

A TRUE BOOK

by

Andrew Santella

Children's Press®
A Division of Scholastic Inc.

New York Toronto London Auckland Sydney
Mexico City New Delhi Hong Kong
Danbury, Connecticut

A Navajo girl
and her goat

Reading Consultant
Nanci R. Vargus, Ed.D.
Primary Multiage Teacher
Decatur Township Schools
Indianapolis, IN

Content Consultant
Dr. Ruth J. Krochock
Archaeologist
Davis, California

*The photograph on the cover
shows two young Navajo girls.
The photograph on the title
page shows a Navajo woman
weaving on a loom.*

Library of Congress Cataloging-in-Publication Data

Santella, Andrew.
   The Navajo / by Andrew Santella.
      p. cm. – (A True book)
   Includes bibliographical references and index.
   Summary: Discusses the Navajo way of life, including their traditions,
legends, families, and homes.
   ISBN 0-516-22503-0 (lib. bdg.)   0-516-26988-7 (pbk.)
   1. Navajo Indians—History—Juvenile literature. 2. Navajo Indians—
Social life and customs—Juvenile literature. [1. Navajo Indians. 2. Indians
of North America—Southwest, New.] 1. Title. II. Series.
E99.N3 S8139 2002
979.1'004972—dc21   2001032298

Contents

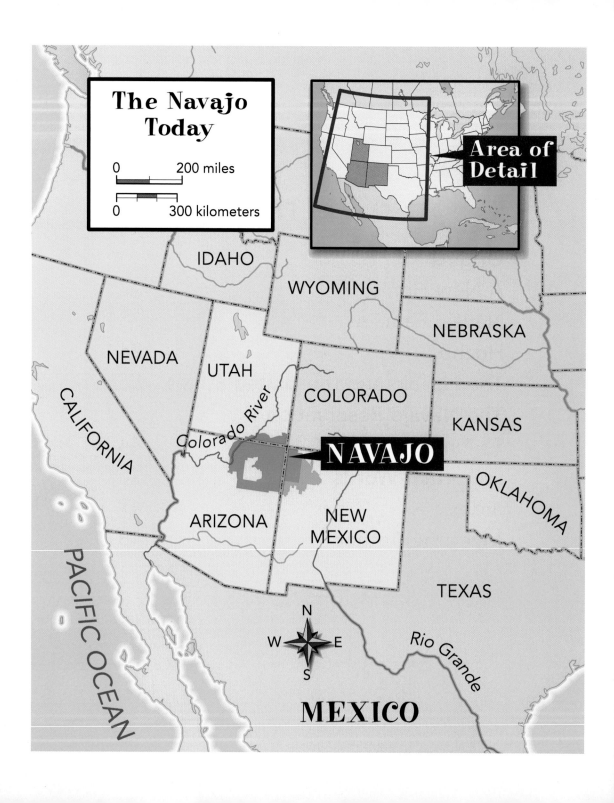

The Navajo Today

0   200 miles

0   300 kilometers

Area of Detail

IDAHO

WYOMING

NEBRASKA

NEVADA

UTAH

COLORADO

KANSAS

CALIFORNIA

Colorado River

NAVAJO

ARIZONA

NEW MEXICO

OKLAHOMA

TEXAS

PACIFIC OCEAN

N
W   E
S

Rio Grande

MEXICO

Origins

Hundreds of years ago, a group of people came to live in the desert of the American southwest. They called themselves simply *Diné* (di NEH) or "the people." Later, Spanish explorers called them *Apache de Nabajo,* which means "Apache of the planted field." This was shortened to Navajo, which is what they are still called today.

The Navajo once lived in what is now northwest Canada. They were **nomads**—people who move around from place to place to find sources of food. Around the year 1000, the Navajo began moving south. Over many years, they made their way down to the desert and settled there.

Navajo **traditions** tell a slightly different story. Navajo

The Navajo found a very different life in the warm, dry desert.

storytellers say that people made their way to the surface of Earth from underground. They say people traveled through three underground worlds. Finally, they arrived at the Fourth World, or the

San Francisco Peaks in Arizona rise above Navajoland to the west.

Glittering World. Spirits called the Holy People, or Yei, told the Navajo to settle in an area surrounded by four mountain peaks. They told the Navajo that as long as they lived there, they would remain safe. The Navajo called this land *Dinétah* (di neh TAH) or "land of the people." Today, some call it Navajoland. Navajoland stretches

A stretch of Navajoland

across parts of Utah, Arizona, and New Mexico. The Navajo **reservation** there is the largest in the United States. To this day, the land on which they live is **sacred** to the Navajo.

The Navajo language is related to the language of the Apache Indians. The Apache and the Navajo may have once been part of the same group. Over the years, the Navajo and Apache developed different ways of life. They became

two distinct people. Today, the Navajo and Apache languages are the only two Athabascan languages spoken in the southwest desert.

A New Home

The Navajo had to adapt to the new world they found in the desert. In the north, they traveled on snowshoes. They also trained dogs to pull sleds. They hunted elk and caribou by driving them into fenced enclosures. Of course, in the desert, there was not much use

The Navajo way of life changed drastically when they moved to the desert.

for snowshoes. Nor did the Navajo find caribou. They did find new ways of life, however.

When they arrived in the desert, the Navajo found other peoples already living there. These were the Pueblo Indian tribes and they lived in **prosperous** villages. At first, the Navajo **raided** the Pueblo tribes for food and property. Over time, they took up farming, just as the Pueblo did. The Navajo began raising corn, beans, squash, and other fruits and vegetables.

Soon they met a group of newcomers. In the 1500s, Spanish explorers and **missionaries** began arriving in the desert. Just as they had with the Pueblo, the Navajo learned new ways of life from the

Spanish. The Navajo received metal tools that made farming easier. They learned to plant new crops such as wheat, potatoes, and peaches. They acquired animals that were new to the desert, such as horses and sheep. Navajo

Navajo first acquired sheep from the Spanish in the 1500s.

weavers used the wool from sheep to make beautiful rugs that are still very valuable today. Even today, many Navajo take pride in their herds of sheep. Weaving is still an important Navajo skill.

Spider Man and Spider Woman

Navajo legends say that Navajo women learned to weave from the Holy People. One of the Holy People was named Spider Man. He taught the Navajo to build looms, which are machines used for weaving. Another of the Holy People, Spider Woman, taught the Navajo to weave.

▲ A grand-mother is teaching her grandchildren to weave.

◁ A mother and daughter spin wool.

Navajo Families

Children are an important part of Navajo society. Navajo mothers carry their children with them while they work. They carry the children in cradleboards—wooden beds with leather straps to keep the children safely secured. The cradleboards allow mothers to

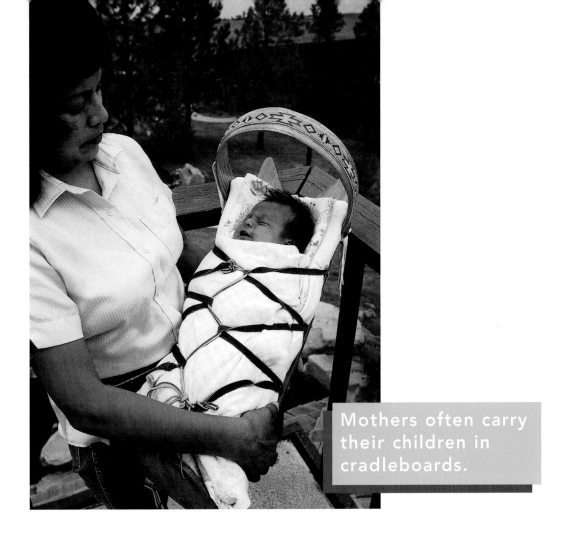

Mothers often carry their children in cradleboards.

keep their children close at all times. This helps strengthen the bond between mother and child. It also allows the children to watch how people work and play with each other. This helps teach the babies what it means to be a Navajo.

Navajo children become members of their mother's clan. A clan is a large group of related people. There are about 60 Navajo clans. Navajo children are raised not only by their parents, but by the entire clan. Aunts, uncles, grandparents, and even brothers and sisters help care for children. Children in

Grandparents usually help to care for their grandchildren (above). Navajo children are playing on a homemade bucking bronco (right).

some traditional Navajo families learn to rise before the sun is up. They are taught to look to the east to greet the rising sun.

The Hogan

The traditional Navajo home is called a hogan (HO gahn). A hogan is a building made of logs and tree branches, sometimes covered with a layer of mud. Storytellers say that the Holy People taught  the Navajo to build hogans. Hogans are still an important part of Navajo life. Even people who don't live in hogans sometimes build them for use in ceremonies. Hogans remind the

Navajo of values that are important to their culture. The logs that form the wall of the hogan are joined together to represent the strong bonds between a husband and wife. The doorway to a hogan always faces east, so that the Navajo can begin each day by greeting the light of the rising sun.

Hozho

The Navajo teach that the world around them is alive and should be treated with respect. They make it their goal to keep the world around them in perfect order. The Navajo word for this perfect order is *hozho* (HO zho). A person's good deeds can help maintain

A young girl helps her mother gather corn from the field.

that order. On the other hand, their thoughtless or cruel actions can destroy the order of nature.

To help restore order, the Navajo perform **rituals** called chants. Chants can be very complex and must be performed by highly trained singers. The Navajo believe that if a chant is performed well, it can win the favor of the Holy People. Then the Holy People will let the Navajo live in order again.

One of the most important Navajo rituals is called the Blessingway. The Blessingway is performed to mark special

One reason a Blessingway is performed is to celebrate the birth of a child.

events like marriage or childbirth. The Blessingway usually begins at sundown and lasts for two nights of singing and praying.

The Navajo and the United States

Settlers from the United States began arriving in the southwest in the early 1800s. In 1848, the United States took over a vast new territory after winning a war with Mexico. Part of the new territory was the Navajo homeland. The Navajo had no

U.S. soldiers clear a Navajo orchard.

say in any of this. First the Navajo were confronted by Spanish missionaries, then by Mexican governors. After 1848, the United States Army tried to control the lives of the Navajo.

The Navajo and the army often came into conflict with each other. In 1849, soldiers killed a Navajo leader named Narbona. Narbona's son-in-law Manuelito rose up to lead a war against the soldiers. Manuelito and the Navajo warriors fought bravely, but they could not defeat the

Ni'hokáá' Diyin Dine'é bi'oodlá' biyi' bitsodizin dóó biyiin dóó bizaad dóó bi'ó'ool'jil hóló éí bee nihidziil. Kodóó dził nihighan sinilígíí bii'ji' bee biih néidzá. Díijidi bee al'aa nídínéet'á. T'áá éí díijidi bee hóldzilgo haz'á. Si'ah Naagháí Bik'eh Hózhóón nidlígo yiildah.

Hózhó Náhasdlíí'
Hózhó Náhasdlíí'
Hózhó Náhasdlíí'
Hózhó Náhasdlíí'

PETERSON ZAH, PRESIDENT OF THE DINÉ NATION
JUNE 01, 1994

A monument marks the Navajo's Long Walk to Bosque Redondo.

U.S. Army. In 1864, the army forced thousands of Navajo to surrender. They made the Navajo march 250 miles (402 kilometers) to Bosque Redondo

in New Mexico. The march
became known as the Long Walk.
It was so awful that many Navajo
died along the way. Those that
made it found only more hard-
ship at Bosque Redondo. They

had to live with the Mescalero Apache, who were enemies of the Navajo. The drinking water there was so unsafe that it made the Navajo sick. The land was too poor to farm.

The Navajo Reservation

Finally, in 1868, the Navajo were allowed to return to their home- land. The U.S. government created a reservation for the Navajo there. In the 1920s, oil was discovered on Navajo land. The Navajo formed a tribal government to deal with the American companies who wanted to use their land.

Oil was discovered on the Navajo
reservation in the 1920s.

Still, the Navajo sometimes suffered from decisions made by the U.S. government. In the 1930s, the government made the Navajo give up many of their sheep. The government believed that the sheep were damaging Navajo farmland.

Government officials were trying to help the Navajo, but they may not have understood how much the Navajo valued their herds of sheep. Today, many Navajo remain angry about the government's actions.

The government took away a large number of the Navajos' sheep in the 1930s.

Code Talkers

▲ Navajo code talkers

▼ The code talkers monument in Phoenix, Arizona

During World War II, a group of Navajo serving in the U.S. Marines invented a secret code based on the Navajo language. They used it to send military messages that the enemy could not read. They came to be called Navajo code talkers. In 1989, a statue honoring the code talkers was erected in Phoenix, Arizona.

The flags of the Navajo Nation, Arizona, and the United States

The Navajo tribal government is modeled on the U.S. government. One of the main concerns for tribal government leaders is education. In 1968, they opened Navajo Community College— the first community college on

Navajo children in Window Rock Elementary School

an Indian reservation. Other Navajo rely on a tribal scholarship fund to attend universities. In recent years, the Navajo have also tried to create schools that would teach Navajo values and traditions.

In many ways, life on the reservation is like life anywhere in America. Navajo shop in malls and eat at fast-food restaurants. However, many

Some Navajo eat at fast-food restaurants on the reservation.

Navajo also preserve their unique traditions. A tradition is a way of thinking or acting that has been passed down from one generation to the next. Educators teach weaving and other traditional crafts in the schools. Healers use traditional methods to help the sick. They believe that the wisdom of the Navajo past will help them meet the challenges of the future.

A father and son keep the Navajo tradition alive.

To Find Out More

Here are some additional resources to help you learn more about the Navajo:

Books

Bial, Raymond. **The Navajo.** Marshall Cavendish, 1998.

Griffin, Lara T. **The Navajo.** Raintree/Steck Vaughn, 2000.

Sneve, Virginia Driving Hawk. **The Navajos.** Holiday House, 1995.

Wood, Leigh Hope. **The Navajo Indians.** Chelsea House, 1991.

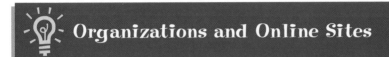

Organizations and Online Sites

Explore the Navajo Nation
www.americanwest.com/ pages/navajo2.htm

A guide for visitors to Navajoland.

Navajo History and Culture
www.lapahie.com/index. html

Information on the traditions and history of the Navajo.

The Navajo Times
www.navajotimes.com

A newspaper web site for the Navajo people.

Important Words

missionaries religious people who travel to new areas to spread their religion

nomad a person who does not have a fixed home and moves from place to place

prosperous very successful

raid a surprise attack to steal money or goods

reservation an area of public land that has been set aside for a group of people to live on

ritual a special way of doing something, often in a ceremony

sacred holy

tradition the handing down of information, beliefs, or customs by word of mouth or example

Index

(**Boldface** page numbers indicate illustrations.)

Meet the Author

Andrew Santella writes for *Gentlemen's Quarterly, the New York Times Book Review*, and other publications. He is also the author of several Children's Press titles.